SPREAD

Through the Fractured Lens of Quarantine

SPREAD
Through the Fractured Lens of Quarantine

Detrick Hughes

Pen & Leaf Press

Published by Pen & Leaf Press

penandleafpress.com

ISBN: 978-1-959743-01-9

Printed in the United States of America

Dedication

1st Sgt. Willie Lee Whittie Sr.

1/4/1948 - 11/14/2020

"In times of stress and danger such as come about as the result of an epidemic, many tragic and cruel phases of human nature are brought out, as well as many brave and unselfish ones."

— **William Crawford Gorgas**
Surgeon General of the U.S. Army (1914-1918)

Table of Contents

Foreword

The world took a deep breath in 2020 as it encountered a ghost of a bygone period, the Spanish Flu of 1918. A similar threat, unseen and insidious, swept across the globe, forcing us into a collective pause. But within this forced stillness, stories continued to unfold. **Spread, a tapestry woven from poems, invites you to step inside** as it chronicles selective events.

These poems are not mere snapshots of a time dominated by headlines. They are observations that delve deeper, capturing the human experience amidst historical shifts. You'll find **echoes of the pandemic's isolating touch**, the fight for justice that surged **across the American experience**, and the ever-present hum of political and racial tension.

But the thread isn't just about the weight of these events. It's also a testament to the resilience of the human spirit. Here, you'll find poems that sing of acts quiet and loud—close and distant. Prepare to be startled, to be comforted, to be discomforted, and most importantly, to be reminded of a shared experience.

This is not simply a book of poems; it's a conversation starter. It's an invitation to remember, to agree, to disagree, to reflect, and perhaps, to find a new perspective on the events that shaped this extraordinary period. As you turn the pages, allow the lines to spark your own thoughts, feelings, and conversations. But remember, **if we are not talking, we are not changing.**

And

Deep in a cruel moment
—felt the marginalized

grow a little silent
—after dudes in laundered suits

formed beasts in collared shirts
to haul their hate-buckets

like empty errand boys
with tiki torches lit

when we heard from the East
a 55-year-old

Hubei[1] fellow fell hard
—assassinated

and labeled victim one.
—Then we were scattered home.

---

[1] The Hubei Province is in Central China.

2020

A Butterfly

In anticipation of a long COVID
—Pilar accepted Scooby Snax[1]

and small red hearts. Prepared a body
as if stuffing it with leaves

where dreams and bodies clutter
an online diary.

Her image cocooned behind doors
became Instagrammed and "liked"

as molting bikini tops, Lululemon
and high heel Louboutin Red Bottoms

are storied. Group selfies fade into deleted folders
with hand-raised colored dixie cups.

You can forget a smile,
but not the way music moved the figure.

Digitized effigies sprouting—her wings
fluttering

under google-glassed images
while wide eyes swipe left, swipe right.

---

[1] "Scooby Snax" is a colloquial term used to refer to methamphetamine, a
highly addictive and dangerous stimulant drug.

About The Wuhan Market?

I leaned briefly holding a smirk
against a racist trope strung carelessly
from "they are stealing our jobs"
to the "kung-flu"
smeared into that snail-shaped organ

then

without amusement
I remember the original birther
spitting into flaming microphones
and unrepentant ears
"I heard he was a terrible student."

so

I guess a birther
by any other name
original or not
could be
just another Bircher[1].

---

[1] "Bircher" refers to a member of the John Birch Society, a U.S. political group
founded in 1958 known for its strong anti-communist views and association
with right-wing conspiracy theories.

And on the 8th Day

God should wake

take Man back

his untamed hand

our frozen lips

that apple rotting

maybe

we were always meant to be plucked

our bodies discarded

collected and reunited with dust

a good life

a less-than-memorable death

but

who knew

narrow dreams

a nibble

would molest fire and water

example

Daddy

made a gun

a baby

and both eventually—screamed

Day 22

Never been friends with death—personally
even when the bastard visited,
I diverted eyes—slightly—pretended
life could be placed on a knick-knack shelf

and retrieved. But when bright lights came
again to the avenue—yelling through panes
and plantation blinds., my bones
waited for those cries,

a sign of life—a REMEMBRANCE
like inscribed on an alter in Beaumont[1]
but sirens remained
closed-mouthed.

They could—would not rise
for the breathless. So,
I—impersonated the living
with a long-ass deep exhale

and some crafted obscenities
quietly hurled at pretty uniforms.
It was not for them. Wanted
their re-used stained gurneys to forget

—the feel of bodies; the cold gaze of pupils
that also
more than once
peered through windows.

---

[1] Beaumont, Texas

Like Crows

I remember dressing in the mornings
between weekends and holidays
when cool air accepted me
after 6:00 AM like a Murder
—or smaller flocks hunting.

We are dying—again
weeding through folktales and reality
while rogue feathered friends
feed on our insecurities
and clean their beaks with conspiracies

after plucking at our eyes.

Passenger

I watched, marred from the backseat
through cloudy windows
where fingertips can stencil letters
—backward

and light bounced
—found its way
through a looking glass
as if running from sound.

I've always known
scattering feet broke that silence
found in the chatter
taken from young men

boasting and singing
and playing the dozens
where familiar streets meet
—scar(r)ing "good" folk.

Government bodies would come
in government cars
with government clubs
to bust some public heads.

But that was before cell phones.

"Recorded?"

"No."

Day 72

"Then stop talking, stop yelling. It takes a heck of a lot of oxygen to talk."
- David Chauvin

Clutching the luxury
to take it back

I held a breath
thirty-some-odd seconds

too heavy to claim
and with no keys

his eight minutes stayed locked,
a lifetime

squeezed through a camera phone.
—And in days buried

we memorialized pixels,
a body,

ganged up on Zoom calls
—stirring

testified to each other
and nitpicked every moment

some realized
—some imagined.

But it laid on skin differently.
In words, it is like piss

saved in a refrigerator
and poured on an open wound.

His glasses lurked just below his hairline
and his uneven smirk lay like pepper spray.

I blink continuously—even now
trying to remove his image.

A hand remains buried in his left pocket
and that badge falls crooked against his chest.

He is my boogieman—the reason
I grip steering-wheels when lights flash.

Political Action Committee

*"We ain't going to burn nothing down. We don't need no foolishness at the
microphone."*
- Unknown Protester

Just to be as clear
as a one-eyed old man
peering through plastic windows,

life is an optical illusion.
Plato
described them as tricks.

Now, like then, country-club men
parade in expensive threads
to conjure monsters and fairytales.

I've never met
an Antifa Revolutionary Rebel,
but I am for Antifascist behavior.

For me—Black Lives Matter
is more of a call
than an organization,

where dues are collected in wicker
from black folks
meeting periodically to take down a system.

It is about the truth
—fresh old bones
buried in songs of freedom.

* * *

My thoughts are loud
as I replace verbal pornography
with leetspeak!

I do not give two f*(ks
that some lady bought a house,
a boat, a car, another house.

Never burned down a city
for a championship or otherwise,
even when a young man took his last breath, but

the 3rd precinct station[1] was destroyed,
and deep in the rubble—I stood
angry at that too.

---

[1] The "3rd precinct station" is a reference to the Minneapolis Minnesota police station that was set on fire during the demonstration protesting the death of George Floyd.

Changing Spaces

On day 79 in Lafayette Square
—I imagined

a protester bleeding cleanly
if one ignores flesh rotting at the first cut

or blood resisting the urge to clot
while crusting on the edge of sidewalks.

Pain becomes artful
if you only remember the flash magazines keep

and you cringe at the way hollering hollows street corners
when wanting begs the flash-bang

and the lean in your walk inspires the rubber bullet
or maybe a knee to the c3

or tear gas
that waits in canisters to transform organs.

Hey, Karen

Delightful to meet you
—and your myth
with its familiar taste

as we were never not acquainted
—these faces
exhumed from crowds

to be lost behind a mask
—changing
or maybe the distance closed

recognizes
—the voice
unmuffled by personality

when another Cooper threatens your dog
—enjoying
a stroll in Central Park.

The Boy from Troy

"Never be afraid to make some noise and get in good trouble, necessary trouble."
- John Lewis (2/21/1940 - 7/17/2020)

John was civil disobedience—the moment repeated
in black and white images like that ragged bandage
—camouflaging a wound awarded in Jackson, Mississippi

or bruises from Bloody Sunday
where Edmund Pettus was memorialized in steel
then nightsticks and blood and tired bodies

that wanted to walk from Selma to Montgomery
and eventually into the civil rights act of '65
across the now—John Lewis Bridge.

Lowered Mask

My smile was caught
in the face of an Asian woman
carrying a visor
that swaddled her head,

and I understood—now,
why the Chinese wore masks
before the pandemic,
as I un-pinched my N95

and she quickly released
my smile.

Signs

Don't mistake me for lonely
even if worry scratches a brow.

I have never sipped from a cup of regret,
and I do not dine on sarcasm.

But sometimes,
honestly,

I miss "the sweet"
or who I wanted her to be,

late when a body echoes cold sweats
and chases the darkness away.

There are unruly moments
when my left hand finds the right

sneaking to remember her skin
and coco butter cream

between the tips of careless fingers.
We are not meant to see,

how easily
we misplace what was tomorrow

while pillowcases become mile markers
for dreamers.

Minimum Wage Doors

A place opened to trade
at 25% in Texas

and a familiar stranger chuckled
slapping a round belly in a booth
creating music for a meal.

The unexpected—
pervades the gap
in a city, any, too full to remember
poverty is a side effect.

Greed and lies
tug the trigger—smokes a friend.
Dying knows no lonely days,

and another body drops,
and we call her essential—
him—essential.

Smile. In a funny way,
the stranger loves you
with that crook captured
in a mouth—exposed.

And still,
we close for business.

Six Feet

I deserted quarantine
for a moment

refusing to stand
with "at least six feet of distance"

by taking a cruel inch forward
and stealing half of it back

—my mask
clutching the smirk.

Cult of Personality (Moon Man)

"It is statistically impossible that the person, me, that led the charge, lost."
- Donald J Trump

When that morning found me
somewhat bare—uncovered,
a man told me he ate the moon.
I laughed. He frowned.

His *"you don't know shit about moons"*
was equally funny and concerning.
Not the words—not the anger
feeding on the bones of downed ships.

It was the passersby
who eagerly gorged on his crumbs.
As the night returned,
a moon appeared

above the collective gasp of bodies.
He told us he created another moon
and we can all eat—yet,
I wept, while other men cheered.

Looking Through Mirrors

Transphobic violence reached a record high in 2020.

Pat placed themselves
tragically at an angle

perpendicular and parallel
as if critical of a new Warhol

before the gunfire
and after their dance with Basquiat.

There is magic in two points
resisting the urge to line up.

No need to add adjectives
or nouns. They are—become

walking sticks evading predation,
the violent beauty of life

some degrees away
from a peaceful decay.

I worried about them both
ignored during but not by a pandemic.

I'm trying to understand
how the non-binary leave

and arrive in the same place.

2021

January 6 Comma

reminded me of Zekes
scaling walls erected around Israel
in World War Z[1].

The infected ignored the infected
breaking glass as if they were the subject
of "The Message"

by Grandmaster Flash and The Furious Five
spitting. But, in a piece of reality,
they were just following

a Don*ald* Quixote.

---

[1] "World War Z" is a 2013 action horror film about a zombie pandemic.

Zombies

On The Day After

We unwound the tape
and slow-struct bodies scattered
out of "the District"
as if the day before was a dark spot
and someone flicked on the light.

We Conferenced

It was not laughter
caught in our throats
when these bodies chuckled in confusion
as we stumbled into other bodies
that had lumbered for ages.

And on the 329th day in reflection

We ate suspicions
that suits stopped listening to the dead
while they were dying and yelling
warming 'selves at burning buildings.

We Understood

Some of the dead
can be given a new life.

The Virus

We hear voices replaced
and we are indifferent, inattentive
as illustrated faces change.

Friends morph and become alien
—unfamiliar in our common spaces.

Koreans become Chinese.

Japanese become Chinese.

Vietnamese become Chinese.

Then the Chinese become
—victimized behind smokey eyes.

Somebody let the quiet out
and the anti-Asian racism
just spread.

If Truth Was That Fairy Tale

The world would not be as blurry
and good men
could open their faces

laugh as racial epithets
rinsed from
big and thin lips

as uninvited folk—could
place their anger in small spaces
that grow smaller

burn the hate as fuel
to chop mountains
like Jimi Hendrix.

Tell babies bedtimes stories
like and about a dude
infamously caught by corners.

Remember, a young man,
 One-eye Jack[1]
who spent his childhood

in a park
in the glow of our beautiful ghetto
black—black

where blades of grass cut knees

----

[1] Donald Ray Smith was nicknamed "One-eye Jack." He lost an eye after being shot with a BB gun.

and stained converted tees.

I watched Jack bury jumpers
on a court of shell and cement—one
glass eye bending a ball

into chain-linked nets
making it sing
old negro spirituals

and enjoy real laughter—hoisted
while playing the dozens.

Photographs and Lies

None of those flat faces blink, but
they bend—the stories
as I thumb through the pages
—finger *The Gram*[1].

An instant message becomes minutes
that linger—remnants of google-glassed flesh
we chase days memorializing
weddings and funerals

as if releasing those butterflies.

---

[1] "The Gram" is a slang reference for the social media platform Instagram.

Dirty Thirty

When we were old,
we sang our stories in reverse

—bore witness
deep in the lazy end of a folding chair

emerging for the summer,
2021, with unused masks

around a drink-stained table
that wobbled

and dragged limp voices
across sandpaper.

We did not run
from sleeping men

leaning into the storm
safe from flying debris,

we shuffled dominoes
and built cuss words

wrapped fingers
around seven or fewer tiles

detached from death
at least for a game of bones

embracing our laughter
and bullshit, two things not killing.

By the Way

The John Lewis Voting Rights Advancement Act passed the House on August 24th of 2021.

Today, remember
John Lewis—the Boy from Troy[1]
—he was *good trouble*!

---

[1] "The Boy from Troy" is the nickname given to John Lewis by the Reverend Martin Luther King, Jr.